On the Way to Putnam

On the Way to Putnam

New, Selected, & Early Poems (1968 – 2021)

Brad Davis

GRAYSON BOOKS
West Hartford, Connecticut
graysonbooks.com

On the Way to Putnam: New, Selected, & Early Poems (1968-2021)
Copyright © 2024 by Brad Davis
Published by Grayson Books
West Hartford, Connecticut
ISBN: 979-8-9888186-7-0
Library of Congress Control Number: 2024904106

Book and Cover Design by Cindy Stewart
Cover Image: View of Putnam Connecticut 1877, Alamy Stock Photo

Poetry collections written or edited by Brad Davis

Short List of Wonders (chapbook)
Though War Break Out
Song of the Drunkards
No Vile Thing
Like Those Who Dream
Opening King David
Self Portrait w/ Disposable Camera (chapbook)
Still Working It Out
Trespassing on the Mount of Olives

Sunken Garden Poetry: 1992-2011 (anthology)

for all who have traveled with Deb and me along the way

Every word ought to carry the meaning that God has given to life (even though it may never refer to God). It ought to carry joy, hope, forgiveness, love, reconciliation, light, and peace in the order of truth.

—Jacques Ellul

Contents

Foreword

I must start with full disclosure: the author of this superb collection studied with me for his MFA, and he remains part of a very small group of truly memorable students after my forty-three years of teaching. So far from disqualifying from commenting on the man's career, however, I believe that having been present at the creation of that career, I can confidently evaluate the trajectory of his poetry from before he was much known beyond a circle of his peers.

As an epigraph to *On the Way to Putnam*, the poet has chosen a passage from sociologist, theologian, poet Jacques Ellul. From the absolute-zero beginning, therefore, he sets the table for the whole collection: *Every word ought to carry the meaning that God has given to life (even though it may never refer to God). It ought to carry joy, hope, forgiveness, love, reconciliation, light, and peace in the order of truth.*

Non-believers may smirk, believers sigh with recognition. Each response, however, will be reductive. While the maker of these poems, both early and late, is clearly a believer, he has conflicting impulses as well: "I'm of two minds," he admits in a new poem,

> one child-like, naïve,
> capable of huge leaps of believing,
> persuaded prayer makes miracles happen;
> the other, well assured nothing matters,
> we being self-deceived, disease-inclined,
> death-destined organisms, full stop.
>
> ("Little River Elegy")

On the Way to Putnam's latest poems candidly consider the ruckus among faith, even childlike faith, good-natured secularism, plain evil, and cynicism. Yet to this extent, those poems continue the central themes and issues of Davis' work from the outset of a noble career.

There's a poem, "Among Luminous Things," in *Though War Break Out* (2005), that I want to quote in full:

In this ocean of ordinary light,
we are reef dwellers. Whether brain coral

or parrot fish or moray, we all do
our bit, then die. The ocean teems entire,

a whole we believe by faith, wrestling
with the darkness and sorrow in our hearts.

I will never regard as wise the fool
who would have me slap a muzzle on

the voice within, small and still, inspiring
praise of whoever it may be who holds

all this in brilliant fullness. I say
let fly with adoration, thanks, and more,

for if this is not the deeper reason
we are here, then there is no reason.

I quote this lovely lyric by way of checking my assertion that, like
all good poets, Davis can keep several ideas at play in the very same
poem without sinking into mere muddle, that among other things,
he never professes simple faith. He must *wrestle* with
countervailing impulses, "the darkness and sorrow in our hearts."
Were he to settle for, or even to feel what in the same volume one
of his neighbors calls "a word from God," he'd be not an inferior
poet, but no poet at all. Of course, he does periodically *long* for an
assurance like that of his neighbor:

Why, unless

my sin were envy, would I begrudge her
an assurance of contact? More likely

I, embarrassed, long for what she has, pained
by my lack of openness to mystery—

which, she has told me, is wholly present
over, through, and in the hedge between us.
                              ("Neighbor as Theologian")

By the time Brad Davis had accomplished *No Vile Thing*
(2008), at mid-career in his aesthetic and personal maturation, he
was in full stride, continuing an arc of achievement that has tended
ever upward. It is not, however, and will not be that he has
banished all the demons that haunt us, believers and skeptics alike.
For one thing, he remains ever more aware that his good fortune is
not available to all, that poets are not exceptional in any way. Their
good fortune, like anyone's, owes itself to factors that have little to
do with their own agency. In "Fishing," a brilliant example among
the new poems, Davis notices that on

> this winter morning
> so much like the last
> the news catches a man kissing
>
> his wife and their teenage son
> goodbye in frigid Bakhmut
> the camera panning
>
> out from the train station
> to a catastrophe
> of rubble where once there were houses

The poet's awareness of his good fortune has remained a
constant from the outset; his awareness of its absence in other lives
is part of what keeps him admirably humble. In the volume
preceding this one, *Trespassing on the Mount of Olives* (2021),
he ruminates on a passage from Luke 22:7, in which Jesus directs
his disciples to an upper room, locale of the Last Supper, saying to
them that, upon entering the gates of the city, "a man carrying a jar
of water will meet you. Follow him to the house that he enters, and
say to the owner of the house, 'The Teacher asks, Where is the guest
room, where I may eat the Passover with my disciples?'" In the
poem entitled, precisely, "Man with Water Jar," Davis finds himself
concerned for the unidentified characters of this passage: it is

15

> the story's unnamed
> who move me—the man with water jar,
>
> his wife waiting up for him, each
> with faith enough to do the next thing
>
> and hope that perhaps their sparrow-like lives
> won't count for nothing—since without
>
> them, their kind, there is no story,
> no reason for the story in the first place.

Such a passage indicates the difference between those, like Davis, who, quite aware of their own limitations, grapple to attend the Teacher's example, and so many contemporary, self-styled religionists who seem intent on celebrating their own putative salvations, taking gleeful note of the ones they're sure are damned, and ignoring the struggles of those with few material comforts.

The author's sense of his good fortune clearly owes much to his wife. "Familiar Spirit," which I won't quote here but which readers should look to an exemplary, and exemplarily *mature* love poem, is among several that pay tribute to his spouse, and his testimony, however understated, is so compelling that somehow one feels Deb's immanence even in work that makes no direct reference to her.

I just used the word *exemplary*, and I'll use it again here. Brad Davis never puts on rose-colored glasses, but from the very start and right through this wonderful book, he does consistently express an exemplary attitude. Over the span of his sustained and sustaining vocation, no matter all the world's deep defects— posturing and deceptions of late capitalist powers, widespread war, starvation, bigotry, hypocrisy, and plain callousness—for him a cautious optimism and an incautious *joie de vivre* and delight in the natural world prevail. But that state of mind had demanded effort. Notice the diction of this passage from "After a Snowfall". "My wish," he says, is

> to hold close the wide, miraculous world I lumber through
> shouting, *There!* and *Over here!* or waving subtly whenever

words or sudden motion might send it fleeing—everywhere
    rejoicing.

Those who accept Auden's dictum that poetry makes nothing happen might consider *On the Way to Putnam*. What happens for me is a strong measure of spiritual refreshment. Davis' poem "Grace Note" celebrates the fact that we,

                the this

and that of us [are] more whole for having
been at the Loft, for having joined

our incomprehensible selves to
the comprehending grace of, well, grace.

Such hard-earned celebration is a profession of faith in and of itself.

Sydney Lea
Poet Laureate of Vermont (2011-2015)
Newbury, Vermont
2024

Preface

With the help of friends—my spouse Deb and poets Bob Cording, Syd Lea, and Don Martin—this collection came together, a five-and-a-half-decade journey with poetry from southwestern Connecticut to northeastern Connecticut by way of Massachusetts, St. John in the USVI, Pennsylvania, Rhode Island, Alabama, Massachusetts (again), New York, Connecticut (again), and Long Island/ Paumanok. A long, strange trip for a Canadian kid from the West Coast.

The earliest poems date from 1968 ("The Ice Harp"), midway through Williston Academy in Easthampton, Massachusetts, to 1991 when I matriculated at Vermont College of Fine Arts for an MFA in Writing. The selected section contains poems from my books published since VCFA, four by Antrim House and two in Cascade Books' Poiema Poetry Series. The new poems are drawn from work completed during three years on Long Island and our first two in Putnam, CT.

After the title poem, the poems proceed from the most recent to the earliest, which might suggest reading from back to front. But however one enters the book, I'm thankful for the visit. I think of *On the Way to Putnam* as a sampler, a testimony to a life of conflicted privilege and modest accomplishment, honest doubt and animating faith—surviving as an artist in a culture that regards the dream of making poems something one needs to wake up from to find a real job.

Speaking of my many employers, I hope they will forgive my never having been totally with their respective programs, whether in the parish or on the campus. Did I, as the old saying goes, steal from Peter to pay Paul? Indeed. Poetry was my first ambition regardless any real job I was getting paid to do—poetry and the contemplative life that comes bundled with it. I hope my employers know that I was always genuinely grateful for their subsidizing of my art practice.

Putnam, Connecticut
February 2024

On the Way to Putnam

Were you to tell him how,
in late summer's

westering light,
his yellow cornfields and,

toward the middle,
that lone, misshapen tree

had become your very own
Serengeti, complete

with buzzards
ascending and descending

upon some bloated corpse,
likely a wildebeest,

Mr. Amaral, a businessman,
would nod politely.

New Poems

Boreal

To speak in English of the north requires words
on loan from Lapland *tundra*, Russia *steppes*,
and Mongolia *taiga*—though *boreal* is Greek.

And early this evening, low over foodie Putnam—
from an Old English personal name *Putta +
ham*, translated *homestead* or *settlement*—

a bald eagle, ordinarily this season somewhere
far from here and normally a boreal breeder
with an appetite for salmon the grizzlies let by.

Eagle: 14th century, from the Old French *egle*.
Salmon: 13th century, from Anglo-French *samoun*.
Grizzly: cognate of Old Frisian *grislik*, "horrible."

And yet not one downtown sidewalk diner
looks up, stops chewing, or covers their grilled,
wild-caught Alaskan sockeye and herbed risotto.

Sockeye: from *sukkegh* in Halkomelem, indigenous
tongue all but silenced by residential schooling.
Risotto: contemporary Italian, from *riso*, "rice."

Familiar Spirit

In the dark, say an hour
before sunrise, when what little light

there is in the room gathers
to the rug's edge and softer lines

of our matching chairs—the floating
lampshade between them—sight

is most like hearing, intimating
presence, these few collected treasures

of a long marriage glad
that I have joined them. Of course,

it is not they who are glad.
Mornings are when light gathers,

whispering her magnificent suggestions.

Little River Elegy

1.

Rublev's angels have no perfection in
and of themselves but only what is lent
them—as it is with all created things:
the oak in the icon, the Little River

below our condo in wooded Putnam,
the cat asleep through the morning's riot
of hummingbirds. Hummingbirds! Like Milton's
rebels angling for the right to rule.

But we are not among the likes of Andrei's
three angels who face and sweetly honor
one another. Our neighbors are Picasso's
troupe of six, stalled in a void where no one

faces anyone. And this is our call:
to be among them as a little river
or sweetwater-filled feeder or as rain—
to be for nurture. Or naught. Have mercy.

2.

Just north of us, a line of stately trees:
broadleaf, coniferous, and here and there
an invasive vine insinuating
with a will to overwhelm the planet.

Do I exaggerate? You judge. I know
only the ease with which I can kill
a wasp or roach or spider trespassing
in my personal space. I am not proud

of this, but well cognizant of devils
among the angels and the need to sweep
a room with martial regularity.
The overreaching vines must be removed.

The line between anger and responsive
stewardship is leaf and litter covered.
I must take care how I investigate
lest, unknowing, I do harm. Have mercy.

3.
I'm of two minds: one child-like, naive,
capable of huge leaps of believing,
persuaded prayer makes miracles happen;
the other, well assured nothing matters,

we being self-deceived, disease-inclined,
death-destined organisms, full stop.
No surprise I love what quiets my thoughts
or overwhelms them: an ocean of ferns

on my thighs like angels' fingers; that view
from the ferry—Rockland to Vinalhaven—
its gallery of glacial art and sea;
even the rush of the elicit—how

for hours, here and there, I can forget
the dissonance tearing at my brain. Best,
it seems, to be a little river free
and clear of all contending narratives.

4.
Life above the Little River is good.
The little river, in and of itself,
is good. As it was created to be.
And there is that of us which is also

good, though we have made a mess of things
and need help to make it right: each other
and, say, wisdom from above. For we are
not as hummingbirds programmed to fight

for food and nesting sites, rather we are
free to work it out peaceably, to dance
and tell self-effacing jokes and linger
quietly around an evening table

and love our so-called enemies. Who would
ever guess this of us, looking at our
histories of war? But why ever look there?
Life above the Little River is good.

5.
In this world, indeed: quartered above
the Little River in busy Putnam,
bivouacked among saints and scoundrels and all
who sleep the sleep of death, going back

to who first encamped along these streams.
Haunt of hummingbirds, the occasional
bobcat, mink, eagle, bear—the place is rich
with life and us, who tip it all toward naught.

O wisdom, here indeed we carry on
for now. From where you sit, I hope to God
our sentience is not irrelevant
or something shortlisted for erasure.

Are you the one to whom prayer should ascend?
I wish only for the good of what is
just and pure—lovely—making no demands.
Only say the word. Only guide our hands.

What to Make of It

Yesterday, walking beside you in Putnam
on the old railroad bed now a trail,
I felt a tad unsteady, slightly
dizzy, as though my brain were not
getting the oxygen it needed.
Today, as I was about my usual
morning routine—a cup of coffee,
the online news—it was not I
who felt wobbly, but the entire
world felt as though it were about to
tip over, break apart, dissolve
into a dizzying mess of lawlessness.
Is there a difference between this
intuition and the irrational hysteria
of yet another conspiracy theory? Might the two
be, by some occult umbilical, related?
This much I know to be true:
I want to feel better having faced
this *affaire du jour*, since later
this afternoon I will kayak beside you
on a still river in northwestern RI,
and dizzy plays out far worse on the water.

American Disconnect

What is it with all the flags
and so many who fly them
enthralled with a wannabe dictator.

(That was not a question.)
But are there not far better things
to concern oneself with

on cloudless October days?
Like the quiet northern section
of the Quaddick Reservoir

above the wooden bridge
along the narrow causeway
where we paddled this morning.

And yet no matter the number
of deer we glimpse or beaver
we follow along the shore

or ducks feeding on pondweed
that we startle into flight, there are,
south of that handsome bridge,

so many flags, so many
flying them on stick-thin poles
from their tidy, narrow porches

and likely furious at our kind
who'd sooner die for a mud turtle
than for him whom they take for a savior.

Fortnight

I've always loved the word "fortnight." From the Old English *fēowertīene niht*, "fourteen nights." A time marker between week and month. The use of it died here in the States. Until the online gaming community brought it back to life, albeit in slang form: "Fortnite."

Some words die quietly as a lily or sparrow and are laid in unmarked graves or left out under a canopy of trees and sky to return to the dust. This one suffered unceremonious digital disinterment, was subjected to violence and made into a monster of its former self.

Which is quite creative, right? I've always admired the vision and skill of the better Frankensteins among us. Have even admired a few of their well-intentioned creations. (Would a list of them help you figure me out? Or are you fine, for now, taking me at my word?)

Speaking of time, I wonder if what happened to *fortnight* is our future, too—and analog life, with its analog meaning and purpose under an analog sun, will be changed, wholly subsumed in the digital continuum and welcomed into deathlessness. Deathless because lifeless.

I'm feeling quite better this morning. Thanks for asking. Temp's normal, aches have fled, slept much better. Though with the increase of hydration has come an increasing need to pee, and my doc, just to be careful, advises I shelter in place a fortnight. A word he did not use.

Mid-Covid

Navy

Small Red

Pinto

Black-Eyed

Baby Lima

Yellow Split

Green Split

Lentil

Great Northern

Black

Large Lima

Red Lentil

Red Kidney

Garbanzo

Bob's 13 Bean Soup
though I count 14
items in the ingredients
a few being peas
and lentils   even so
I love the nod
to prime   the irony
of that so-called
unlucky number
paired with so much
flatulent goodness
just add water   ham bone
and slow cook all day
season to taste

Old Man Poem

There are whole days I swear I smell something
like auto exhaust in the dry air of our condo,
a scent you say you've not picked up on,
and I get suspicious of how tired I become
mid-afternoons or when I try to read before bed.
Most of those days I pass it off as an effect
of Covid or the swim workouts I continue
to put myself through. But today was different.

Today my eyelids grew heavy in late morning
as I was reading online this NPR article
about the hazards of poor indoor air circulation
notably for the elderly, a population to which
apparently we now belong, and especially in homes,
condos, and apartments with gas appliances—
which is indeed the case here at Sabin Landing
where we've landed following retirement.

But what is this poem really about? Because
so far all it sounds like is the worry of an old man
who, with all kinds of time on his hands,
has fallen prey to mortality anxiety, fearful
of anything that could contribute to cutting short
his momentary fling under a generous sun.
You say this "piece" fails to sing like a proper poem.
I say look how it bears a faint, stanzaic resemblance to one.

Sunday News

After two days of heavy rain
along the Natchaug, Diana's Pool
(named, some say, for a suicide)
was all aboil. We arrived at noon
hoping for the whitewater kayakers
we'd heard wait for this water.
But either it was too early

in the season, or the first arrivals
deemed it too dangerous and
pushed out a note to the network
of other crazies we went out to see.
So we settled for a leisurely negative
ion fix, witnessing the happiest
water south and west of Putnam.

Happiest, that is, until we returned
to town where our Quinebaug
over Cargill Falls was roiling
like a Pentecostal congregation
in the grip of a Holy Ghost anointing.
Even the Little River was feeling it,
a little. And so today, though oil

prices climb and stocks tumble
and the virus claims another few
thousand, these happy spring waters
amped by heavy rain preach
our homily, giving voice to an old
story that's a rollicking antidote
for all the recent woes of the world.

It's Complicated

We've neighbors I've never seen who
have two dogs. I only know this
because every time the neighbor
lets them out to take shits,
he feels he needs to yell their names

over and over to get them to quit
our two yards' wooded boundary
and come in. I'd mention the dogs' names
but if he found out I told you
about them and how he carries on,

I worry his political yard-signs could
animate, become physically threatening.
Some days, especially those
when his yelling at them turns profane,
I worry for the child whose sweet voice is

an apple petal on a turbulent sea.
The only name the neighbor calls the child
is "Buddy," but as it's what he'll call
a dog when trying to be nice,
I suspect Buddy's not the child's name either.

A while back I think I passed the neighbor
walking one of his dogs on our road.
More like I saw a dog walking a man.
Thought then about the child, too. Couldn't help it.
Chose not to pull over and introduce myself.

Wintering in Putnam

Though there are those
who give the slip to these

parts, opting for a warmer
southern clime as we

hunker here in Putnam,
we are by no means left

alone to bear the season's
bitter brunt. Why, just

this morning, the high, bare
branches out behind our

condo shimmered with
juncos, chickadees, wrens—

flitting flashes of fine
resistance, unpersuaded of

the migratory argument.
Neither revolutionary

nor religious but feathered,
an economy of druthers

encoded in the hollow
of their bones and beaks,

they winter here close by,
their eye on us, ours on them.

Fishing

from a painting so titled by Jean Wetta

1.
so much like the last
this winter morning in Putnam
flickers on the suet

so unlike Bakhmut
where no boy I know
wakes to an air raid siren

not one makes plans
to go ice fishing
or to a movie with friends

2.
the painted lake nearly glass
boat engine off
this year's vacation so

much like the last
though you are taller
shoulders broader

your sidearm cast
out beyond mine   yours
no longer your mother's voice

3.
but this winter morning
so much like the last
the news catches a man kissing

his wife and their teenage son
goodbye in frigid Bakhmut
the camera panning

out from the train station
to a catastrophe
of rubble where once were houses

4.
like mine in Putnam
and where a woman sits
in her pitted driveway

watching pigeons go about
their daft business
cooing   sure of nothing

atop the roof now an island
in a vast flooded lake
of smoking brick and timber

Of All Places

Stony Brook, NY

Track lighting on the wall art.
On the twenty or so tables,
lumpy orange, votive-lit globes.

A line of gentle spots halo
the opening guitar trio's shuffle
along the moment's precarious edge.

This is Wednesday night, The Jazz Loft,
which is neither the Gaza Strip
nor the Fuzzy Grape or some

pricy urban food emporium.
Here the stage is overseen
by a crouched, furious Catamount

stuffed and perched above
the freight elevator. And if I know
nothing else, I know why I am here,

how being in this blue room—
stir in keys, a trumpet, sax, that slide
trombone—delivers us (a moment) from evil.

The Suit

Pressed between the prospect
of swung eighth notes
and the delicate waltz of pastels,

this hour is a heretofore
unworn suit of clothes, the room
a form, a frame, a chart, plain

white paper, and each tune's
harmonic structure is the given
we all play over, repeating ourselves,

it seems, in unending variations
on the same old same old—
the point being to praise or lament,

to slip our voices, our bodies into this new
suit, as though it were tailored for us.

Grace Note

Another week here and the light
wears a second shirt—the air

more dry than cool—and the night's
royal blue hair falls like, well,

blue hair across the soft shoulders
of whatever this is, whatever

we are making new, now, together.
Within these walls, under these

lights, we "bring it" (as they say)—
re-membering our humanity—the this

and that of us more whole for having
been at the Loft, for having joined

our incomprehensible selves to
the comprehending grace of, well, grace.

At Sea

Stable format and platform dissolve,
your line unspools—think

bonefish or bluefin—and you
are at sea under a waning moon,

the last of your kind day-
dreaming a continental wish of

landfall, and if you think you imagine
you know where you are (or

where I am), lay back on the broad
main, infinite heaven above you,

and forget the old systematic
longing for coordinates; certainty

of one's whereabouts is a child's cartoon.
Either we are or we are not upheld.

Rishon

Genesis 1:3-5

Before the candle or star field—light
with no local source.

Like a water wash laid on cotton
paper to prepare for the painting's colors—

or like, say, the time feel
Paul Chambers ascended into

before that first inevitable take
of "So What"—light

before the governing lights
determined the old light/dark divide.

And as in the emptiest spaces of the cosmos,
so too in us, even at our emptiest—

light, inextinguishable
mode of all being—the visible and

the invisible—light long before critters
and beds and familiar shadows

or my waking to another
morning of a rumored resurrection,

that first crazy take
on where all things may be headed.

Shlishi

Genesis 1:9-13

to get wheat—land

to get land—the waters
gathered into seas

to get the waters—seems
they arrived   with
earth   formlessemptydark
when nothing was   but the deep
and the surface thereof

to get the vault of sky—the separation
of waters above   from
those below

to get the lights up   beyond the vault—first
a thinning of the waters above   then
(like an eye opening)
a break   in the clouds   then
many more   propitious breaks

to get that thinning   those many
propitious breaks—the whole
earth set to cool

to get it cool—ask Bird
or Trane or Monk or Ray

to get it right—Miles

My Last Night at the Loft

and the room's on life support.

Fewer than ten of us,
including the trio and model.

I'm not superstitious, but pulling
for the musicians,

I switched to an Irish red ale,
and damned if now,

tune by tune, they're not painting

the empty corners
of this blue room a brilliant red.

Selected Poems

from

TRESPASSING ON THE MOUNT OF OLIVES (2021)

Credo

for my father

He is disappearing from himself.
She is learning to spend time

away from him, out with new friends
for dinner, a show, a nightcap.

He does not know that he was left
with a nurse to feed him his lasagna.

He does not recognize the fork.
And on the far side of

a wall he hasn't a clue is there,
his whole life waits to be returned

to him—in the resurrection, a bit
of nonsense I believe because the idea

is beautiful: *What is sown mortal
will be raised immortal.*

Man with Water Jar
Mark 14:12-14

1.
If you look carefully
in the painting's lower left quarter,

just inside the Essene Gate
of the Old City,

you can make out a man
cradling a child-sized water jar.

Milling around him are several women,
their jars balanced

on their shoulders or heads.
The street teems with commerce

and red-caped Roman soldiers
and all manner of priestly comings and goings

to and from the Temple courts.
An ordinary day in the City of Peace,

except there's that man—and two travelers
entering the city who will follow the jar

to a house and a room upstairs in the house
where they will see to it that all is ready.

2.
What does the man cradling
the water jar know of the Teacher?

Given a need for secrecy,
he would not have heard the Teacher

instruct the women to tell the homeowner
to prepare his upper room for *Pesach*.

Likely all the man knows is nothing
more than where to stand and how

to hold the jar and to be watching
for two Galileans who will enter the city

as though looking for someone. Likely
the man is indentured or enslaved—

reliable as the homeowner is
trustworthy—and wants nothing

more than to discharge this duty
and return to his own family by nightfall.

3.
Form fitted to function, class,
and proximity to source;

whether hewn stone or shaped clay,
stitched hide or banded wood—

long before ascending
from the earth of domesticity

to the paradise of metaphor,
the water jar

enabled entire civilizations
their rise and prospering.

So we all are indebted to what-
and whoever delivers us

our daily *dour, ura, ama,*
vatn, tskhali, nero, wai, mmiri,

uisce, thuk, av, aiga, aegoa, amazi,
dlo, d^wr, voda, uisge, water.

4.
But fetching the water
was a servant woman's work;

a manservant's to receive it from her
and distribute as instructed.

Was there shame in being a man
standing with a water jar

near a principal gate
of the holy nation's royal city?

May we assume—and why
not—the manservant suffered

his ordeal for a benefit sufficient
to buoy him through that long afternoon—

something inscrutable
unfolding?

5.
They are the story's unnamed
who move me—the man with water jar,

his wife waiting up for him, each
with faith enough to do the next thing

and hope that perhaps their sparrow-like lives
won't count for nothing—since without

them, their kind, there is no story,
no reason for the story in the first place.

Judas of the Suburbs

Who rises early
to birdsong aiming

to get it all wrong? Even
evildoers feed the cat,

make coffee for visiting in-laws,
sing to themselves

and in the congregation
hymns of a better world—*soon*

and very soon—a balanced
ledger, vindication.

Not every beautiful
brown bird that alights

in the crabapple
can be a waxwing.

My Two Bits

Luke 24:36-42

You don't know me. No reason you should.
Yet when he asked,
I was the one who served him

the broiled fish I had prepared for the others.
Nothing out of the ordinary.
And when he spooned my fish into his mouth,

I started laughing, something I did
whenever he did the strange, wonderful things he did—
and the men would shush me

and send me on ahead to find a well
or scout out a place for the night.
Sometimes the men were like that with us,

but never the Teacher. He had this way
of speaking to us and including us in the work
that I don't think he mentioned to the men.

So when he received the bowl from my shaking hand,
I knew he was no ghost—and this time
no one shushed my laughter,

for we were all laughing and crying at once.
Even the Teacher,
who had somehow come back to us.

The Generative Influence of Q on John's Gospel

The fragment is on the mark.
Whoever wrote it down got it right,
and I should know.

From a boat offshore,
my younger self watched it happen:
the crowd pressing upon the Teacher
as he taught on the beach;
he commandeering Peter's boat
and telling him to put out into deep water;
we rolling our eyes
when he instructed Peter to let down his net,
yet then having to help him land
that crazy haul of fish;
and finally back on the beach, the Teacher
announcing, *from now on, you will catch men.*

Ever since it was entrusted to me,
I have treasured this fragment,
holding it as first among the other fragments
I keep rolled in a scrap of leather.
And there's a new reason I hold it dear.

Early last Sabbath, the rains dampening
my eagerness for eldership here in Ephesus,
I unrolled the fragment
to refresh my sense of commissioning—
you will catch men—
when suddenly the words
turned themselves inside out
and I became dizzy, like that day
in the upper room with the Spirit-fire.
Suddenly the crowd on the beach
listening to Jesus teach the word of God

became a crowd on a beach
listening to God.
I felt myself melt, as if into a glorious light.

Then later in the day words occurred to me—
In the beginning was the Word,
and the Word was—
along with a compulsion
to write them down
and follow them with other words.
And it was as though I were once again
following Jesus up some rocky path
between small towns on the way to Jerusalem.

I'm telling this to all of you
because the idea these words convey
will be called blasphemous.
I may suffer for having written them.
But I know and trust their source,
and when I'm done they must
be sent around to all the Teacher's friends.
Which makes me nervous
how even they will receive them,
for none of the others have spoken as plainly
of the Teacher in this way—
as the great I AM. So I have awakened you,
the moon still bright above the city,
because I want you to sit with me and pray
as I write what I will write.

You know how tired I become by early afternoon,
and how I have needed your help
shepherding our little flock here in Ephesus.
Well, now I will need you even more
to help complete the new work. Please,
someone bring me my pen, ink, and parchment.

from

STILL WORKING IT OUT (2014)

Gardiner Creek

They, who preach the world
is mine to make, exhaust me.

As though without me—or
someone sadly like me—there is

no epic tale of light's procession here,
no narrative of tides

or of desiring birds. Is this
what they, over breakfast,

tell their children?
Out here, in dawn's half-light,

where the creek makes me whole—us
whole—I praise the narrow inlet,

its brackish story, that warbler nearby
getting it said—*I am here.*

Quietly

The snow continues to fall.
When she joins me
I will build a fire we will keep
through the afternoon
into evening. This is how we live.
The logs will burn down;
she will grade exams on the couch;
I will read Wendell Berry
or the Iliad or finish a new
song I've been revising
since the turn of the year.
It really is like this.
If we go out for dinner,
it will be with friends
whose daughter just had a baby,
no self-conscious flourishes
of cleverness, no
flamboyant posing as avant-garde.
Our lives have meaning
we do not make for ourselves,
or have to. It is a gift,
like the falling snow and this time
to get our work done.

How to Wait for the Second Coming

Dust and vacuum, because the light
is already here. Between shaking out

this throw rug and that, reverence
the forsythia. Sounds crazy, but bake

rounds of shortcake for the neighbors.
Tie a blue ribbon on the one

you will give to the unhappy widower
who lied to you and yelled at your kids.

At work, spend equal time
with random coworkers and breathe

slowly, savoring each breath the way
you savor each course of a holiday meal.

This is the gift he sends before he comes.

Father Nicholas

Tuesday
Week of the Sunday closest to June 1

All four seasons in that same wool cassock, always at six & slowly, every weekday morning down the far side of Bay Street, Nicholas walks through town.

I remember his first boat—we were ten—& the old, twenty-five horsepower motor his father bought from mine. All spring after school he worked on it, sanding off the old paint, refitting the seats & oarlocks, anticipating the rub of rope on gunwale, the first spiny, green haul of lobster in a boat of his own. For hours, perched on a stump outside their barn-like garage, I'd watch, & whenever I inquired into what he was doing, he'd answer, hardly looking up.

All four seasons on each return trip from the bakery by the causeway, Nicholas cradles a long white bag of hot bread. Dr. Morse, the pharmacist, tells me I make too much of Father's routine. Says we all concoct formulas for getting by. I say, while he walks, Father prays silently for each & every one of us—& every morning as he passes opposite my rooms above the old five-&-dime, I cross myself.

•

Friday
Week of the Sunday closest to June 29

Devotion, Father's been fond of telling us lately, has more to do with courage than piety, & without fail, I hear again my own father's voice lecturing my mother & me—over Brahms—of passion, sacrifice, & the necessity of routine. I don't think my father ever worried I'd become fearful of him. Still, after each lecture he'd take me for a ride into town to the docks, & we'd watch the gulls hover off the backsides of trawlers. I knew it was my time for asking questions &, on the drive home, ice cream at Bailey's.

I never, till now, doubted Father's word, & even now, it's not that I don't believe it's true. It's that I doubt devotion is anything most of us in the parish have even a passing interest in, like lizards or the southwest. We love the idea of one of us, plain & simple, vested, arms outstretched between brass candlesticks, bearing our world boldly to the throne of grace—& so long as he continues to make us feel welcome, loved & treasured here, he could accomplish nothing else, believe no more than we do, & we'd keep the rectory in good repair forever.

•

Monday
Week of the Sunday closest to July 6

As a child I thrived on leather-bound books the size of pulpit Bibles. I imagined my father the world's authority on such collectibles, & for years kept completely secret the ritual I watched him perform most every evening as I tiptoed past the study to the bathroom.

He kept his collection in two large oak & glass cases he bought at auction the summer the jeweler went bankrupt. Lifting a volume, like an egg from a nest, he'd set it down on the plush red pillow atop the counter, adore it as he did my well-rounded mother, & in one smooth, deliberate motion, bend at the waist until his face, eyes closed, hovered cloud-like, nose inside an inch of the broad, calfskin plain. Two long, deep draughts & only then would he straighten, adjust his eyeglasses, & actually open the thing.

Each morning, for months after he died, I practiced the rite, inventing gestures of my own over the little red book of prayers & poems mother'd bought for me & inscribed with a fancy pen—*on the occasion of your first communion.*

•

Sunday
Proper 10, Closest to July 13

When Nicholas' mother was hospitalized for the last time, I visited her weekly. Kept her up on the doings around town. Toward the end, once I knew she couldn't see my father's likeness in my eyes, or hear clearly my mother's tongue on mine, I asked her—though certainly not before the usual to & fro of newsy chatter—if her son had ever expressed an interest in the ladies. I told her, from what I heard tell, the Harris girl'd been keen on him a while, but she'd never say yes if he never asked. *No,* she replied softly, *he's never dated.*

After she died, Nicholas halved the number of his lobster pots. Started splitting the extra time between fixing things for anyone who asked & heading off upstate every third weekend for what we later learned were appointments with the bishop. I never did believe the rumors, & each time he went away, I'd swing by her gravesite Saturdays after breakfast & set out new flowers, just so, at the foot of that smooth, pink-ribboned stone he'd ordered special from Italy.

•

Monday
Week of the Sunday closest to July 20

Twenty years ago today Nicholas' mother died. A full five before the bishop talked him into selling his boat & lobster pots & laying traps for men. I remember that sermon. The whole town turned out. Priests from all up & down the state rolled in to lay their hands on him. Yanked him into orders, just like that. You should have seen his face pinch in the receiving line when an old, leaf-dry deacon knelt down right then & there to beg of him his first priestly blessing. Only priest I ever met who makes robes look manly.

His first couple months as pastor were (I shouldn't say it, but it's a matter of public fact) fun for us. The bishop hadn't required him to go away for seminary. Said his age & the parish situation qualified him for an exemption that, in this case, he was more than happy to grant. So when it came time for Father's first mass, he swung the incense like he was throwing a buoy overboard. Had us all in stitches with his awkward cadences & muffled cusses each time he lost his place. No question, the acolytes had the hardest go of it. But by Christmas we'd grown accustomed to him, & by Easter, I couldn't imagine anything sweeter than taking the Body on my tongue from his large, right hand.

•

Thursday
Week of the Sunday closest to August 3

Nicholas learned how to work wood from keeping those pots, but it gave me pause last Saturday afternoon. I was letting the dog run when I came upon a small, glass-faced cabin the parish secretary later told me Father'd built for personal retreats in the wooded, northeast corner of the church property. The door had no lock that I could see, so I entered.

The room was spare. A kneeler at the center faced out through the plate glass. A leather Bible open to Ecclesiastes lay beside a journal on a lectern. Against the north wall, an eye-level platform bed, desk & chair directly beneath, & in between, chiseled in caps across a three-foot length of oiled cedar & mounted on the knotty pine wall, *Create in Me a Clean Heart, O God.*

Like a child in a neighbor's tree fort, I don't remember breathing, & left without disturbing a thing.

•

Wednesday evening
Week of the Sunday closest to August 10

A windless heat wave landed on us yesterday, & Mother's words ring in my ears: *Until the weather breaks, shop early & keep purchases to a minimum.* So I shopped this morning for the three-speed window fan cooling me as I write. Then tomorrow, up to Boston. Asked for these days back in June, so heat or no heat, I'm city-bound. Good news: the radio says storms will bring relief over the weekend. Had the car washed & gassed—all set for an early departure. Mustn't forget, on the way home, to pick up a present for Nicholas—his fiftieth—& speaking of our priest, from where I sit, it seems he's gone missing. Dr. Morse says I'm overreacting. Maybe so. Either way, I really must get some sleep. The new fan should help.

•

August 15
Feast of St. Mary the Virgin

Wednesday a week ago, after three days not seeing him over breakfast & before leaving for Boston, I called around. Best I could tell, I was the first to raise the question of his whereabouts. Not even the parish secretary thought anything of it.

Thursday the harbor master left a long message on my machine: said Monday at dawn he'd taxied Nicholas out to the *Sursum Corda* & watched from the dock the tidy ketch tack neatly into mist beyond the chop. Mondays are Father's Day off. Said he remembered him mumble something about a mystic center in mercy, like it were a destination Down East or something—which is when my machine cut him off.

Sunday the diocese sent a priest on holiday from the Midwest to read the liturgy. After the sermon, I slipped out through the side door of the nave & made for the little cabin behind the fellowship hall.

Yesterday Dr. Morse offered me a job at the pharmacy to keep his books & pay the bills—& I began taking flowers to Nicholas' mother's grave again. He never did get used to us calling him Father.

Every morning at breakfast, to remind me whose I am, I still cross myself. He'll be back. Then, one day when he needs me, when he asks for me by his bedside, I'll be there for him, like I've always been, from the beginning—& I'll touch everything.

Washing Dishes After the Feast

It frightens me to think, she said, interrupting
my holiday banter. Imagining the phrase
as antecedent to a rare gift of honest exchange
between grownup siblings, I dashed
into the split-second of dead air, anticipating silently
her elaboration—*what a mess we've made of things*
for our kids; how many parents of starving
children must hate us for our amazing prosperity
and self-indulgence.
      But I had misread
her punctuation, took the period as a pause, and all
at once found myself, like that coyote
we used to pull for on Saturday mornings, utterly
without purchase, eyeballing an abyss.
Which is when, glancing back across the divide
of the double sink at her busy hands, I saw her
as though she were curled in a ball on the lip
of a cliff, knees tight to her chest, face buried
in the cotton folds of a holly-green dress.
It's okay, I wanted to tell her. *It scares me, too.*
But I was already plummeting, tumbling in free-fall
to a sunbaked canyon floor, the crazy cur
in her endless cartoon of an unreliable universe.

from

LIKE THOSE WHO DREAM (2008)

Good Things

At the Met, hundreds of instruments locked
behind bulletproof glass—Segovia's

among them—cold as a photograph.
When I get home, Bill will be dropping by

whose life, one year beyond Donna's slow
dying, has begun to open into what is,

for him, a familiar direction. For years
the road was his destination of choice:

bars, honky-tonks, county fairs; *anywhere,*
any time, any amount; every now

and then a real music hall, a listening
crowd with sober ears who cared how he voiced

the light, bending twang of his pedal steel.
Just back from the first tour in a decade—

eight shows in eight nights, from Cincinnati
to Atlanta—Bill says he has stories.

So I'm guessing, over coffee we'll do
a fair bit of laughing, settle into

that crazy sense of knowing why we're here,
then maybe say a prayer or two before

he returns to an empty apartment
and I flick the toggle on my Blues Junior,

wait for the tubes to begin to glow, and send
the first notes of a new song spinning.

Google *Robin Needham*

for Lucy

Your e-mail's subject line read *Clearing*.
(How soon will this language be obsolete?)

I pictured the six of you arm-in-arm
outside your home in Katmandu, mountains

over your shoulders, the latest monsoon
making a welcome but fitful exit.

Here, a half-dozen chimney swifts cavort
above my neighbors' roof, oblivious

to the suffering you have called home
for three decades, your tent pitched among

refugees—Kampuchea, Bangladesh,
Kenya—your witness, even through the years

we lost touch, an icon of the good dream.
You are moving again, and while clearing

out boxes from closets, you found my letter,
dated, and new e-mail address and so

thought to bring me up to speed. Has it been
a year since I wrote to you? But then

your second paragraph. I had to read it
three times before I could receive its news:

the six of you on holiday in Thailand,
the twins and boys trading laugh-out-loud tales

of college life and school in Chiang Mai, all
settled in at Golden Buddha Beach.

Which is when, like Herod's goons in Bedlam,
the Christmas tsunami tore into you.

"Life is strange," you wrote. "The children ran
for their lives. I survived. And Robin, well,

google *Robin Needham*." So I did.
Now, in these ridiculous lines—his body

found after five days by Nat, your oldest,
a full kilometer into the jungle—I

cut a path through the dense tangle of crap
in my psyche to the wide-open place

where all our long silences—wanted
and unwanted—converge and embrace.

Common as Air

When Mrs. Weiss told us in earth science,
a light, limb-filtered breeze blessing us
through the room's west wall windows,
that somewhere camouflaged within
our every lung-full of air marches air

Hitler breathed and Khrushchev and
Richard Speck, I began breathing less—
shorter intakes, pauses after each exhale—
willing to endure panicky bursts of craving
in exchange for reducing the likelihood

of those radioactive atoms passing
from lung to blood to brain. If she included
mention of the Buddha or Madame Curie,
I do not remember it. Terror is air-borne.
And though I have been slow to believe,

so are wisdom and beauty, the breath
of canticle and rain forest, and in such
measure as dwarfs the one or two
dark, burrowing parts per million of all
that is our phenomenal inheritance. How

I wish now a teacher had told us that this
is the reason, when we hyperventilate,
we get so dizzy—so much goodness
flooding our little brains it very nearly
bowls us over, tips us toward our knees.

At the St. Francis Yacht Club

To my left, Golden Gate; right, Alcatraz;
Sausalito, straight out across the bay.

Here protests are polite formalities
filed with a rotating race committee,

and I'm weak-kneed before Olympic gold,
framed press releases, action photos

of spinnakers, crews, square-jawed skippers.
Suffering here is elective, like prayer

or wondering what on earth St. Francis
would make of a yacht club that bears his name.

But I'm here for a wedding reception—
to *A-men* love and a nine-piece funk band—

and not to rule against the darling couple
in matching yellow rain slickers. Not now.

Procession

An unbroken line, more a river
        of starlings passed over the library
                courtyard, my fresh coffee going cold,

and just as it seemed the last
        pilgrim had straggled by, another wave,
                hundreds, no thousands more cleared

the treetops, streaming into view,
        their chatter ecstatic—for twenty minutes
                running—wave after wave after wave.

A bad day would make of them a figure
        for how *dismal* never seems to quit:
                word after word of shootings, suicides,

the heart's upwelling—felt as never ending—
        of raunch, revenge, temptations to silence
                conscience, do whatever damn well pleases.

But they are birds, not emblems.
        They did not arise from my dismal heart.
                They do not regard me as significant,

even less themselves. Their regard reserved
        for the ineffable *amen* moving in each
                that moves them all to join the long flight south.

from

NO VILE THING (2008)

Enough

Luke 22:47-51

In a garden, one word, and a new way bursts
open in the redneck heart of a fisherman,

an old accessory of war falls, dropped
beside a severed ear, and God in the mayhem

stoops to take up again not the sword
but the ear and attend to the wounded.

Ever since God told Abraham
that He is not a deity who desires the death

of a child, the change was in the works.
And now here, in a garden,

with one word God reconstitutes
the modus operandi of his people on earth.

In an instant, blood-weariness blossoms
into rebuke—*Enough!*—and to make example

to the strong and weak, the brave and bitter
of this world, God lays down his arms.

My Spiritual Practice

When I sit still in my office for ten minutes,
the lights turn themselves off. I love being

overlooked first by the lights' motion sensors,
then by those who assume I would not choose

to sit alone in a darkened room. They pass by
looking for me elsewhere. I do not care

to be seen by anyone. I am never tempted to wave
an arm and trip the affirmational switch.

Invisibility suits me. I enjoy imagining others
deciding I must be out sick or on an errand

or that finally I've delivered on my threat: to buy
a one-way bus ticket anywhere south and west

of this office in this suburban private school
where, several times a day, I make the lights go out.

The Good Life According to *Architectural Digest*

In a tall, open-walled poolside pagoda,
      suspended from teak rafters smooth as marble,
          saffron curtains like festal banners descend

in waves from a sweeping, hand-carved canopy
      that once topped a Buddhist temple in Thailand.
          So much for reverence in south Florida.

Some days I want out of this modern mishmash,
      this hang-loose apotheosis of the *au courant*.
          But where to go? The same

irreverence travels with me, clings to my every
      move like Spanish moss in the live oaks surrounding
          the redeployed pagoda, and I want

that pool house, pool, those lawns and live oaks,
      the uniformed staff of twenty-five smiling Cubans
          who minister like spirits to the elect of God.

Genuine Replications

The pitch in the subject line being for neither
pharmaceuticals nor porn but watches,
this morning I decided to open the spam.
Good news: the watches are not those fake
knock-offs any tourist can pick up cheap
on a big-city sidewalk, but honest-to-goodness
replicas, authentic pieces of jewelry that cost
a tad more, but you know what you're paying for:
peace of mind, that feeling you know and trust.
Language is not the enemy here anymore
than industry is the enemy or government.
When I consider the immense and terrible
perfection of a class-five hurricane, the purity
of a tsunami, or a quark's thrilling song and dance,
I do not comprehend how anything perverse
ever could have evolved anywhere in the universe.
That you and I exist at all makes no sense:
from primal forces dumb as the chair I sit on
rises sentient personality? Not likely.
And not just sentient but sniveling and self-
absorbed, arrogant and pathologically cruel.
Explain this: I feel ashamed of my own kind.
Some humans are even bored, determined,
it would seem, to prove that they are also stupid.
On some mornings it is easier to believe
nonsense will resolve into meaning and God
will pay back the wicked what they deserve.
But this is not one of those mornings.

After a Snowfall

Above a shapeless field, the fine, up-swept tip of a redtail's wing.
On an unplowed road, euphoria at spotting it suddenly.
Then later over tea, delight in recalling the moment's perfection.
And now this.
    If all were mere necessity, then why such beauty?
We are perhaps the only witness to what we think we see
and long to enter—a sacred grove, a new earth, a father's well-
prepared welcome home—and so leave behind all want, all sorrow
for what never fails to spoil our truest effort.
         My wish:
to hold close the wide, miraculous world I lumber through
shouting, *There!* and *Over here!* or waving subtly whenever
words or sudden motion might send it fleeing—everywhere
  rejoicing.

from

SONG OF THE DRUNKARDS (2007)

Waiting

With no enduring city here, no
homestead or ancestral cemetery
to ground a sense of belonging,

what reaches in to shape a vision
is beauty. Hey, it's everywhere:
not only in lakes and flower gardens,

but peeking over a Kmart facade
and slanting off parking lot puddles.
Compositions abound, planned

or haphazard, that leak the news:
*yes, here, too, beauty tabernacles
among us*—the way an abandoned

shopping cart points to the white
Salvation Army donation bin
and, beyond, toward a stand of trees

hung with crows crowding
the lot's perimeter. Salvation. Now
there's a beautiful rumor: that I may

trade-in my load of moral pain, my fear
of being found out and shamed,
and right away recover a bit of what

I most want to see more of:
the beauty of holiness.
     Here,

stationed solo on the paved crown
of this hill, parked and waiting
for my family, I follow the crows'

jerky line of flight as they rise up
from their rain-darkened perches
and set out for nowhere in particular.

On the Balcony of the Racquet & Tennis Club

Psalm 57:4

Between potted plants—the pots hewn from blocks
of granite the size of small cars, the plants
Babylonian—he considers how to bend
light around himself, become
nothing or, if not nothing,
then nothing more than
a mid-air peripheral shimmer
in their visual field who hobnob
at this Park Avenue landmark; he imagines
becoming something spectral, nothing
actually to pursue as he was obliged to pursue
the invitation his boss pressed upon him
to enjoy this mid-week, mid-town bash
at the racquet club and these petite
crab cakes, broad tables of champagne,
skewered scallops. Being overwhelmed by
even the loveliest of phenomena
is not the same as being filled with goods things—
Mary's *agathon*—without which even the wealthiest
roll home *kenous*—empty-handed—
behind their snappy, black-capped chauffeurs.
He knows her Magnificat by heart.
Knows, too, that these in their heels
and silk ties—MBAs and Doctorates
of Jurisprudence—these, too—their memberships
like inviolate kinship bonds—mask
with smooth, articulate elegance
lives common as rice and beans.
Here on the thin margin of this
open-air balcony, between tall, leafy exotics,
he thinks slowly to himself that he has forgotten
so much of his life, and those here
cannot help him remember it.
But he does not care that they cannot. He cares only

that in the morning he will wake up
beside his wife, and they will make a day
for themselves that they will likely
not remember ten or five or, hell, one year
from now. He is not sure anymore
that he even wants to remember his life,
for it would take too many interviews
with too many strangers who would swear
it had been with him that this
or that vivid memory of theirs was made, and how
could he refute it? For now
he wants only to bend the porch
light, city light, star and moonlight, all light
around himself and make good,
from this loveliest of clubs, an unseen exit.

Judgment

Bones are good. Any fool knows
        it's bad to be drawn, bone from bone,
                and quartered.

Scatter the bones of fools,
        and you spoil their best chance
                at finding rest.

Some fools, appealing to God,
        strap explosives to their skin,
                make shrapnel of their bones.

Still, the good of bones abides.
        Even in clever fools
                who know to dress up

their corruption in charity,
        each of their bones is good
                as the moon is good, or old growth,

or the vulture I saw—hollow
        boned—a hundred feet above
                the doughnut shop in Dayville.

Anticipating Our Retirement

Her plan: to visit forty-plus friends per year,
one friend a week for as many puttering years
as we may be welcomed by them. After that—
for, one by one, they will die or refuse our calls—
we will lay claim quietly to public lands:
interstate rest stops, state parks, scenic overlooks,
national seashores and wilderness areas, you name it.
This is her vision for finishing as we began,
debt-free and future-bound. No doubt you have
heard it said, "Birds have their Soho lofts;
foxes their waterfront condos." True, and true.
But we will finish up here having only the wheels
that will bear us gloriously from point A to point B.
My part: to choose the model, make, and color.

Then

she knocked and without waiting entered.
      Then she tried to speak.
           Then she
apologized and reported that
      a plane had flown into
           the World Trade Center,
a tower had fallen, and another
      plane had crashed into the Pentagon.
           Then she left the room.
Then without having to be told
      I canceled the rest of class,
           and without having to be told
we walked together to the auditorium
      where, without having to be told,
           everyone had begun to gather.
Then I saw my wife arrive
      with her class, and from across
           the auditorium I knew we were both
thinking about our son.
      Then the trustees conference room
           became a communication center.
Then dozens of students and teachers
      donated the use of their cell phones.
           Then dozens of students and teachers
started dialing and redialing nonstop
      trying to reach family in New York City.
           Then our son,
keeping musicians hours in New York City,
      awoke. Then he dressed
           and walked up West 51st Street
to get coffee. Then crossing 8th Avenue
      he looked south
           at smoke rising over lower Manhattan.

Then my call made it through
        to our son in New York City
                as he stood without coffee
on 8th Avenue looking south.
        Then I tried to speak.
           Then I apologized.
Then I passed the cell phone to the next person.

from

THOUGH WAR BREAK OUT (2005)

Crossing the Williamsburg Bridge

Easter Morning

Walt Whitman's Brooklyn behind us, we are walking
to Manhattan and a late brunch in Chinatown:

steamed dumplings, rooster sauce, pan-fried sesame bread,
plastic bowls of spicy mushroom soup, oolong tea.

We walk above traffic, the river; beside the JMZ line,
share elevated pedestrian lanes with cyclists, Hassidim,

speed walkers, hippies, Latinos, arty types in all black.
You are here—a mantra learned from maps on kiosks

in suburban malls—plays in my head, and softly (to myself)
I offer up an Easter hymn under Jerusalem-blue skies.

All families will bow before him; he is the King of glory.
To the south, a thin column of cloud rises like altar smoke.

The earth is the Lord's, and the fullness thereof.
In this light, even the jaded skyline stands transfigured.

Neighbor as Theologian

How can she talk about a "word from God"?
The weather, yes, or the fate of our hedge.

A snake or the shrinking odds of her spouse
beating cancer, sure. But a word from God?

As though God were an actual person,
albeit incomprehensibly vast.

Yet this is how she talks, the way I talk
about my son from whom I could never

hear too much or too often, who's only
hours away in Brooklyn. Why, unless

my sin were envy, would I begrudge her
an assurance of contact? More likely

I, embarrassed, long for what she has, pained
by my lack of openness to mystery—

which, she has told me, is wholly present
over, through, and in the hedge between us.

Eucharist

Never have I felt a natural draw
to work anywhere close to an altar,

though, with this loose pile of sticks laid neatly
on a bare patch of earth, the ambition

to live quietly, minding my business,
becomes oblation, an ordinary

work of hands in service to grace. No priest
required, no victim, knife, or temple tax.

To this ground may a sweet, heavenly fire
descend. Here, where air sickens with the stench

of war and the perfunctory smoke
of religious ceremony, I turn—

keep us safe, O Lord our God—
to collect windfall for the coming night.

Crossing the Notch

for Deb

In tight, fast-wicking garb and hiking boots,
he looked like someone who would know

how much farther we had
to where the Long Trail met the notch road,

so when he told us we were nowhere near
and would need to retrace our slow

steps back up and across the icy ridge,
our sweat-soaked cotton clothes grew heavier.

Knees failing us, even the light breeze
of a late-October mid-afternoon became

an enemy plotting our ruin, and in that
trail-side exchange, our hike

revealed itself as pure folly, potentially dire.
Who, O Lord, is not a novice, an amateur

in this business of setting out and arriving?
So progress came down to a bushwhacker's

word versus the confidence of us flatlanders
in a cryptic text on a trailhead sign

and occasional glimpses of thin white blazes.
Finally, we pushed past him

and, inside a descending hour, found
ourselves—despite the grand indifference

of a shadowless day in northern Vermont—
safely on the narrow road through the notch.

Among Luminous Things

In this ocean of ordinary light,
we are reef dwellers. Whether brain coral

or parrot fish or moray, we all do
our bit, then die. The ocean teems entire,

a whole we believe by faith, wrestling
with the darkness and sorrow in our hearts.

I will never regard as wise the fool
who would have me slap a muzzle on

the voice within, small and still, inspiring
praise of whoever it may be who holds

all this in brilliant fullness. I say
let fly with adoration, thanks, and more,

for if this is not the deeper reason
we are here, then there is no reason.

Early Poems

How to Read Criticism

as
metaphor   as

left
guessing
right   figuring

Pegasus   by abacus
reaching in-

to cookie jars   to finger
what is

better tasted   tongued
than fiddled with

Even Stars Collapse

Even stars collapse, fold in
upon themselves, like raisins.

Having served one universe,
they are reassigned, removed

like a dog-eared book of prayers
from my bed table to yours.

And what is loss here, is gain—
what is here a dense, dark hole,

is a nova's brilliant splash
in the deep space of elsewhere,

dazzling astronomers,
sending spasms of sheer awe

to the ends of a new realm:
a new heaven, a new earth.

Bio

Wilburn Parley-Valencia's third
and fourth collections,
Quizkid's Revenge and *Greywater*,
brought out recently
by the Hysterical Lute Press
and reviewed in this issue,
are thematically contiguous
with his forthcoming novel, *Mas Senhor*,
to be released in Brazil by an
as yet undisclosed publishing firm.

Born in Caracas, raised
in Pasadena, schooled
in Kansas and New York,
he is presently poet-in-residence
at Fremantle Community College
just outside Perth, Australia,
where he is a contributing editor
for an Italian yachting magazine
and covering the pre-race preparations
for the 10-meter "Australia's Cup."

He has been married "frequently"
and claims to "have known some happiness
in those miserable years."
He is now living "a marvelously
sensuous existence" with
"a small bevy of very soft, very
elegant men and women of various hue
and dubious repute" on an "exquisitely private"
multi-unit compound on Cape Naturaliste
overlooking Geographe Bay.

Parley-Valencia's first collection,
Notes from an Expatriate,

was awarded, in the award's
inaugural year, the Yellow Rose Prize
for excellence in Hispanic-American poetry
by the El Paso Committee
for the Advancement of Hispanic-American Art.
He writes, "albeit guardedly,"
that his last round of chemotherapy "seems
to have done some good, though only time will tell."

A Domesticated Eschatology

Lightbulbs disappoint.

With each change
the crazy hope occurs,
however subliminally—
this may be the last.

With diapers, likewise.

Yet, someday,
the doing of diapers
will cease
(thy saints shall bless thee)—

and, one day,
even lightbulbs
will be redundant;

the Lamb will shine forever.

Time

1.
It is a familiar town
frequently duplicated:
a circumstantial place-name
with nothing to boast of, save
a local Latin scholar.
All's well there, and seasonal,
and even the Murphy boy's
found a wife and five acres.
But all that's behind us now.
Memoirs and tombstones remain,
and a dark, somnolent drawer
of yellowed wills and titles.
It is a town in repose:
a peaceable settlement.

2.
It is an endless movement
and ubiquitous besides:
a domed, steady state of flux
where, with martial oversight,
a river never freezes,
never thaws, never reaches
the sea without corruption.
One prospers here. Another,
silent as fire (as winter)
shivers, dreams, picks through the waste
and eyes the rolling caissons.
It is a restless movement:
a migration of peoples
predisposed to wandering.

3.
It is a vast continent
and varied: a land imbued
with undecaying grandeur,
a wilderness of plenty,
though we may not settle there.
We may not build our cities
on its riverbanks, or plow
its fertile plains and valleys.
It is not ours to exploit,
not ours even to explore.
It is a far, fleeing place
our circumstantial poets
cannot see: a land possessed
by no one, promised to none.

After Working Late

St. John, U.S. Virgin Islands

The double yellow lines were invisible,
though by some faint, empyrean glow, what we could see
were the even deeper shadows on either side
of the road's gently sloping crown.

All along our slow climb up Caneel Hill
we could hear them—imagine their wing spans, the faces
of the giant fruit bats that flew with us—
their swooping, airy rhythms just above our heads.

Yet not once as we plied that harrowing
black channel of asphalt home,
did a single, bug-eyed flying fox mistake us, hand
in hand, for mango, lime, or papaya.

Nerve-addling angels of our island nights—
we came to think of them as porpoises off our anxious bow
and welcome their company, strange comfort
on our slow ascents from the hotel, after working late.

Nature

On occasion through boyhood
she bundled me in her skirts

and spun me about gaily
making me dizzy with glee.

I remember loving her
in those times and always will,

no doubt, prefer her roundness
to the square patterns of town.

But now, like a distant aunt,
I see her more in photos

or daydreams than face to face—
and think I hear her laughter

sometimes in early evening
between sips of tasteless tea.

Noel

Cornered by swirling
      second-story waltzers, a flashy
            brass quintet oom-pah-pahs

as outside a flurry fumes, wind-
      whipped into mocking
            funnels and drifts. Below,

blowing into cupped hands
      like a virtuoso, a pretzel man
            bobs a nimble jig beside

his shiny metal pretzel stand,
      anticipating tips from home-
            headed out-of-towners—

as the flakes, glittering
      in the gleam of street lamps,
            pay no mind to the vendor's

blue umbrella and vanish
      with barely audible hisses
            over the steaming pushcart.

Steel and Sleep

The rail is kin to the girder, the rivet, the gun—and not without the bitter pain of a thousand miner's widows, or the weary work-gang songs of hope and a good night's sleep, did he catalog America's early miracles of steel.

The nation burgeoned—the city scaled Jenney's ladder to the clouds (Mumford's *iron cage* and *curtain wall: colossal: paleotechnic*), and he was child enough to love and hate it all, but not enough to simply shy away.

If ever a poet embraced the shovel's slave and cursed the orey pit, it was Sandburg—and over the graves of the driven dead he said his iron eulogies then rose to mingle with the land, the people, to raise his fierce and bitter voice,

stained with the hope of driven hands, in songs of steel and sleep.

For Something More

a song lyric

children
laughing lightly daily linger
on the sand
watched by animated nannies
who fuss about the horseplay at hand
and hurry when the big wind and the rain cloud
roll in

children
soon to grow and bound to wonder
bound to cry
asking adolescent questions
they listen to the hit tunes and sigh
laugh only when the sun comes and the school day
is done

children
gone from laughing days of horseplay
gone from sighs
left with naughty little children all their own...
they lose themselves in memories
and die

One Day

the brick will burst the mortar
    the beggar buy the house

the sheep will keep the shepherd
    the lion feed the flock

the price will pay the debtor
    the widow bless the priest

the sun will shade the alley
    the grave forgive the gun

Blue Sky Grave

a song lyric

sitting in the morning
mindless of the creeping cold
wondering
if anything is everything grown old

sitting in the morning
pitching dreams against the curb
wondering
if everything is just another word

sitting in the morning
torn between the day and night
wondering
if anything is easier than right

Once Upon a Coffee Table

A golden lion stared
From his perch
Curious,
Not the least bit scared

At the whittled countenance
Of a wooden madonna
Standing
In the sterling pond.

"An humble woman, she,"
Thought he,
"To be among such
Company."

But, alas, the cat was made
of brass, and she
Of splintered sighs, had eyes
for me.

Bridges

Bridges, gleaming steel and cable,
rivets flashing in the sun,
slowly rise from asphalt beaches
reaching toward unguarded skyways
where the winds as rivers run.

Down, suspended from high heaven,
millions surging at their feet,
bridges, bending so—like rainbows—
condescend with grace and slowly
distant asphalt beaches meet.

If

it does not explode
poetry is useless

Close the Doors

and windows.
i've had my fill
of your shit.

to hell with
appointments
to see you.

what do you care
for the i
in my head—

all that i keep
safe from you
stashed

in my ego closet
for burial
with my name.

i am. i lives
in me.
till parted by death.

[toad]

toad, earth-brown, warted,
quivering in tight green eyes

Keeping Time

the Black dancer strides
into the world
side by side with brothers
and sisters

keeping time

the Black dancer moves
hard and fast
across the world
with beautiful
furious brothers and sisters

keeping time

the beautiful dancer leads
with long legs
black and powerful
into the world
side by side with striding sisters
and brothers

keeping time
keeping Black time

The Ice Harp

Winter days and nights that year were cold
but not enough to freeze a pond from edge to edge—
and I, a pleasant day ago,
while walking by the pond,
cast a stone upon the ice.
At first I though a bird in fright
had chirped and flown away.
But then upon a second stone
the chirp returned and I,
so taken by the simple music,
cast my stick aside
and entered into twenty minutes throwing stones
upon the thinly frozen crystal drum.

Notes

In the New Poems section, the poems between and inclusive of "Of All Places" and "My Last Night at the Loft" were drafted during my three years on Long Island in New York. All of them had their beginnings at a weekly evening session, The Art of Jazz, held at The Jazz Loft in Stony Brook during which writers, painters, and jazz musicians worked simultaneously in the Loft's performance space. In that dimly lighted room, it was a gift, while drafting these poems, to be listening to live improvised music, watching artists sketch and paint from a clothed model, and noticing my fellow writers' heads angled toward their glowing screens.

Among the Jazz Loft poems, the two entitled "Rishon" and "Shlishi" are from a sequence of seven poems, one for each of the seven days of creation found in the first chapter of Genesis. *Rishon* translates as "first" and *shlishi* as "third."

All the poems selected from *Trespassing on the Mount of Olives* and the Antrim House collections—*Though War Break Out, Song of the Drunkards, No Vile Thing,* and *Like Those Who Dream*— build from a slow read of the Gospels and Psalms, respectively. The publisher of *On the Way to Putnam* felt that some of the poems require a mention of their triggering verses, so I've included the verses as epigraphs. For the poems in the Selected section that stand without a scriptural epigraph, their triggering verses are found in their respective collections.

Section 1 of the poem "Man with Water Jar" is an ekphrastic on a painting that I invented so that I could describe it. I was inspired by those wonderful *Where's Waldo?* cartoons, and the paintings of Bosch and the Bruegels.

In "The Generative Influence of Q on John's Gospel," the "Q" in the title refers to "a hypothetical Greek-language proto-Gospel that might have been in circulation in written form about the time of the composition of the Synoptic Gospels." (britannica.com) The "Q" refers to the German word for "source"—*quelle*. The scrap of text referred to in the poem I imagine as having been circulating independently, prior to finding its way into the hypothetical proto-Gospel named "Q."

In the "Father Nicholas" prose poem sequence, the time markers at the head of each entry are from the Book of Common Prayer and correspond to days in the Christian calendar.

Like the book as a whole, the poems in the Early section read from the later poems to the earlier.

About the Author

Brad Davis (MFA, Vermont College of Fine Arts; MDiv, Trinity Episcopal School for Ministry) is a California-born Canadian living in northeastern Connecticut, where, in 2022, he was a Writer-in-Residence at Trail Wood, the Edwin Way Teale homestead and Audubon property in Hampton, Connecticut. Author of ten poetry collections, Davis' poems have appeared in *Paris Review*, *Poetry*, *Connecticut River Review*, *Image*, *Michigan Quarterly Review*, *Here*, *Spiritus*, *JAMA*, *Brilliant Corners*, *Connecticut Review*, and many other journals in the United States, Canada, and England. Awards include an AWP Intro Journal Award, Sunken Garden Poetry Prize, and numerous Pushcart nominations. He has taught at two colleges (College of the Holy Cross, Eastern Connecticut State University) and two boarding schools (Pomfret School, The Stony Brook School). He lives with his spouse in Putnam, Connecticut, on the traditional lands of the Nipmuc Nation now based in South Grafton, Massachusetts.

Acknowledgments

Though responsibility for these selections is mine, the four wonderful friends mentioned in my preface contributed immeasurably to culling the herd, and I owe them a debt of love. As well, I have abiding gratitude for those who first accepted for publication the poems included in this volume:

Anglican Theological Review: At the St. Francis Yacht Club

Ascent: Eucharist

Assisi: At Sea, Rishon

Brilliant Corners: Of All Places, The Suit, Grace Note, Shlishi, My Last Night at the Loft

catholicliteraryarts.org: Fishing

City Works: The Good Life According to Architectural Digest, Judgment

Connecticut Review: Genuine Replications

The Cresset: How to Read Criticism

EcoTheo Review: Gardiner Creek

Ekstasis: The Generative Influence of Q on John's Gospel

Here: Familiar Spirit, Old Man Poem

HIS Magazine: Even Stars Collapse, Bio, A Domesticated Eschatology

Icarus: Father Nicholas (sections 2, 5, 6, 8)

Image: Common as Air

JAMA, Journal of the American Medical Association: Credo

Kingdom Poets: Sunday News

Louisville Review: Anticipating Our Retirement

Main Street Rag: Crossing the Williamsburg Bridge

Mockingbird: Father Nicholas (section 1)

Newport Review: Time

Paris Review: Washing Dishes After the Feast

Poetry: On the Way to Putnam

Rock & Sling: Judas of the Suburbs

Sanctuary (Journal of the Massachusetts Audubon Society): Procession

St. Katherine Review: Father Nicholas (section 3)

Solum Literary Journal: Man with Water Jar

Tar River Poetry: Waiting, Neighbor as Theologian

Willimantic Chronicle: It's Complicated, Nature

Wolf Den Review: After Working Late

Also:

• Of the early poems, from "The Ice Harp" (1968) through "Nature" (1976), several were printed in high school and college literary magazines.

• "Bridges" (paired with three photographs) won the 1970 Charles E. Rouse Creativity Prize from Williston Academy.

• "Good Things" and "After a Snowfall" first appeared in the chapbook, **Short List of Wonders** (2005), winner of the 2004 Sunken Garden Poetry Prize.

• "The Procession" won the 2009 International Arts Movement poetry contest.

• "Washing Dishes After the Feast," "Common as Air," and "On the Way to Putnam" appeared in **Self Portrait w/ Disposable Camera** (2012), finalist in the Black River chapbook competition and the White Eagle Coffee Store chapbook contest.

• "After a Snowfall" appeared in the anthology **The Turning Aside** (2016).

• "At Sea" was a finalist for the 2020 Vallum Award for Poetry.

• "At Sea," "Of All Places," "The Suit," "Grace Note," "Shlishi," and "My Last Night at the Loft" appeared in the chapbook, **Of All Places**, finalist for the 2020 Elyse Wolf Prize.

- "Little River Elegy" appeared in the anthology *Waking Up to the Earth* (2021)
- "Fishing" was runner-up for the 2022 Catholic Literary Arts Sacred Poetry Contest.
- "Crossing the Williamsburg Bridge" appeared in *The Ellul Forum* (2024).